JOURNEY FROM PAIN TO PURPOSE

STACEY J. TURNER

JOURNEY FROM PAIN TO PURPOSE

Stacey J. Turner

Published 2022 by

SJT Publishing Co.

Copyright © No. 1-11191759261

Printed in the United States of America

ISBN: 978-0-578-38011-7

Table of Contents

Acknowledgments

I like to take this time to acknowledge my Spiritual Dad, Apostle Kelvin J. Newton, for all of his spiritual guidance, correction, and Agape Love.

Apostle Rosemary Haynes, thank you for your fire that helps me catch fire to my Ma. You pulled out of me what was hidden, and you help to cultivate that God has placed way down deep in me, and for that, I love you! I know I am a force to be reckoned with, but so are you. There were many days we collided with one another because we are a mirror image of each other in many ways, not all but a lot. Thank you for hanging in there with me and not throwing in the towel. Thank you for being my biggest cheerleader!! Love you lots!!

To Apostle and Mama Hodge, Thank you for introducing me to Jesus, teaching me Jesus, and showing me how to honor Him with my new life in Him. Thank you!!

Lynn Taylor Jordan, I love you more than you could ever know to my dearly beloved sister. Keep the faith!!

Pastor Don Middleton I thank you for your obedience to God in changing your prayer and asking God to save someone from that club across the street from your job and then shut it down. I thank God for honoring your prayer. I am saved today because of it!! God bless you exceedingly and abundantly above all you can ask or think.

Introduction

Journey from Pain to Purpose was written to help others affected by sexual abuse. It lets others know that there is hope, healing, and deliverance in Jesus Christ, the Saviour of the world! It shows how He can clean you up, and you never look like what you have been through. Jesus leaves no residue. He does a complete job from the inside out if we want Him to. If we let God through the washing of His Word, we can become a masterpiece, an original, one of a kind!

The importance of this book is to let others know of the unfailing love of Jesus Christ. No matter where you are in life, if you give the life you have to Jesus, he can work miracles with it as long as we agree with him and his word.

The content of this book walks you through where God found me, how He reached out to me to draw me to himself, and how I fully committed myself to his will and plan for my life. There were many deliverance sessions, and there are still more happening and more to come because we are all battling something in our lives that only God can heal.

Chapter One

My Journey Begins

This journey began in 1969 when I was born In Harlem, NY, to Katherine and Eddie Turner. It was the year of Black Woodstock, a series of music concerts held in Harlem, Manhattan, New York City to celebrate African American music and culture and to promote the continued politics of Black Pride. Genres: R&B, soul music, jazz, pop, and rock were played in Mount Morris Park in Harlem. I was the fourth child of Katherine and the middle child of three of Eddie Turner.

Shortly after that, Mom found work in Bridgeport, Connecticut, so we re-located when I was 10 months old; according to the story, my mom told me when I asked how we got to Bridgeport, Ct when I was born in N.Y.? She told me how the doctors had given her a due date of December 6 for me to be born. However, Christmas came and went, New Year's came and went, and I was still in the sack. So, my mother said she "walked the floors trying to push me out. I drank a 1/5 of liquor trying to push you out." In those days, you could smoke and drink in hospitals; It wasn't until the early eighties that doctors figured out cigarettes give you cancer, so they put a stop to smoking in public places like hospitals and airports and on airplanes by 1988. Even before birth, when you are destined, the enemy will try and kill you through ignorance and bad choices, but I'm here to tell the story.

In the summer of the year 1978. I had a good life. I had everything I thought I wanted for a nine-year-old except a bicycle which my mother would never buy because of fear of me getting hit by a car. I had skates, a skateboard, board games, a jump rope, food, clothing and shelter, and friends on the block that I played with just about every day. What more could I ask for? So, I was happy. I had no complaints except for wanting a bicycle cause all my friends had one. I never did get a bicycle, even though my next-door neighbor taught me how to ride on hers.

We lived in a two-family house with a first-floor apt and a second-floor apt. We lived on the second floor from my second earliest memories. It was a lovely day outside, but my friends were away from home with their families, so I didn't have anybody to play with this particular day, so I played alone on the front porch. It was common for neighbors to come over on the porch and play as I went to their front porch to play from time to time, so there was no alarm for my neighbor to come and play with me. However, this play day would change my life forever. As my teenage neighbor and I played, he took me to the back of the house, where he pulled my pants down and sexually assaulted me. After what felt like a long time, He left me in the backyard. I pulled up my clothes and ran into the house to the bathroom. As I used the bathroom, I felt fear come over me, and I was so afraid I told no one.

I don't remember how much time passed before I used the bathroom and had the burning sensation that made me almost scream aloud. Still, I couldn't because I was too scared and didn't know what to say about what had happened to me. It hurt so bad, but I was too scared to tell my mom or anyone what had happened to me. So, I lived with it in silence. Even though I knew something was wrong, I never told anyone. Fall rolled around, and I never told a teacher, another student, or a principal. Absolutely nobody. I went through the school year with a secret that I couldn't tell anyone about.

The following summer, the 4th of July weekend, at age 10, I began my menstrual cycle for the very first me. My mother discovered I had my menstrual cycle because I put my panties in the dirty clothes hamper, and she washed all the laundry. I wasn't allowed to operate the washing machine yet. My mom called her mother, who was living in Louisville, Kentucky, at the time to tell her of the beginning of my period. My grandmother cried, saying, "she's still a baby." When I found that out, I really had to hide my secret. I couldn't let that get out too. Oh my God! I felt like I wanted to hide and never be found. I buried it even further within myself. No one knew, so I had to keep acting like nothing ever happened.

This baby was developing into a grown woman on the outside while staying a silent child on the Inside. It was the weekend because I didn't have school and my mom wasn't working. She wasn't at home either. When my stepfather came into my bedroom as I was asleep, he crawled into my bed and raped me. I was scared and didn't know what to do or say. I tried to play dead by lying as still as possible and ignoring what he was saying about my mother while raping me. The following day, I ran bath water wanting to wash it all away as if it were a dream and I would wake up from it. As I'm bathing, my stepfather comes into the bathroom and begins to self-pleasure and ejaculate in the bathwater I'm bathing in. I reach for the towel to get out of the tub.

Again, I never told a living soul about what had happened because I was afraid and couldn't believe this was happening to me again. As for my mother, I found out later that she had a side boyfriend she would visit on weekends, which is how I became prey. I felt like nothing. I was very empty inside and couldn't articulate what had happened. I felt cursed because these bad things had happened to me.

Shortly after that, my stepfather was gone, he moved out, and I was relieved. I would be home alone and loved it. This was when I became very withdrawn. I didn't want to play with my friends anymore. I used to play with my neighbors and just stopped without any explanation. Being home alone, I didn't have to talk to anyone, so it was effortless to keep these secrets. We lived on the second floor, and I'm home alone, and there's a knock on the door. My downstairs neighbor's husband came upstairs and knocked on the door, and asked me to go to the store for him. I would go to the store for his wife all the time, so no problem.

I went downstairs to get the money from him to go to the store, and he began to pull me to the floor as he sat on the sofa, I knew what was about to happen, and I pulled away and ran back upstairs. We were taught not to disrespect adults in those days, so I never said anything to discredit him or any adult. I was a child. Children were seen and not heard. I continued to go to the store for the wife, and one particular day the husband was home. He goes back downstairs to retrieve the money.

As she was handing me the money, he was standing there looking at him, and I felt anger, and it must have shown on my face because the wife said to me, "why are you looking at him with a mean face"? So I took the money and went to the store. Needless to say, I still said nothing.

Chapter Two

It Didn't Kill Me

It's now 1981, and I'm 12, and my grandmother moves from Louisville, Ky, to live with my mom and me. My sister and brothers had moved out with their girlfriends. My sister had moved to Orlando, Florida, and I still haven't told anyone about what happened to me. Mom is working full-time, and Grandma stays home to care for the household. God came and visited me early, telling me what He has called me to do for Him. I never told anyone that either. Grandma went to church every time the doors were open, and I went too. During a week's revival, a prophet prophesied everything God told me he wanted me to do for Him, except he prophesied it to my sister, who was visiting and standing next to me in church, and I was in shock. He said everything correctly, just to the wrong person. I didn't know anything about prophecies, so I stood there very still staring at him as he prophesied, thinking to myself, He knows everything God said to me...WOW. I never told anyone about God visiting me, not even grandma. As grandma began cooking, laundry, and cleaning, she saw the heavy discharge in my underwear. Grandma asks me about my underwear. I was in complete shock that she even noticed, and I had not thought about what to say. I just buried the shame, pain, and hurt deep down inside of me. Even at her questioning me, I said nothing. I would just stand there feeling numb, not knowing what to say.

Eighth grade rolls around, 1983, and I'm now 14, and we are in biology class learning about the human body, how it functions, and where babies come from. Although in the course, we were also taught about STDs (Sexually Transmitted Disease) and how they are transmitted, which is where I first learned, I had been given an STD and the cause of the burning sensation I had from the onset and every so often after that. That, too, I suppressed.

Having spent years suppressing rape, sexual assault, and having an STD, I felt like can anyone see my pain. No one could see my pain, and I couldn't even at age 14 tell anyone.

Grandma had moved into the brand new senior citizen building, and mom and I were alone. Mom went to work, and I went to school trying to fit in and be a (typical) teenager. I became angry because no one could see. I began to give my teacher a hard time at the beginning of the school year, only to suppress it so I wouldn't land in hot water and have to explain why I was misbehaving. If Mom had to take a day from work for me cutting up in school, I would have gotten a beat down. So, I knew I had to straighten up.

The hot water was turned off in the house. My mom could not afford all the bills with just her income, so my mother and I moved into the worst project in the nation, according to the USA Today news article I had read. We went from a house to living in the projects, and I transferred to a new high school. Ugh, how much more could happen within me. By age 17, I was very suicidal, wanting to kill myself. Home alone, I would sit on the arm of my mom's chair, contemplating how I was going to kill myself.

I had made an open vow I would never forgive the people who had done those horrible things to me. Still, I would always hear, "if you killed yourself today, how would you know your answer isn't in tomorrow"? I didn't know at the time that the HOLY GHOST was ministering to me. I was angry because no one ever knew what I had been through or was going through, or at least it was never spoken or heard of, so I felt like I was the only one, and why me? I distinctly remember a voice that said, "commit suicide, you're an alcoholic, drink, you're a lesbian, do drugs."

I kept hearing it and didn't know what to do. I did all I could to resist. I would cry, my eyes red, but I would always hear, "if you killed yourself today, how would you know your answer isn't in tomorrow"? That gave me hope to see the next day. I didn't have it in me to hold a gun in my hands. I wasn't going to slit my own wrist and see my own blood. Pills didn't even cross my mind, not that we had any anyway. I became very hard-hearted. So, when an adult tried to tell me what to do, I was very rebellious and didn't want to do what they said because my attitude was, where were you when I needed help and how are you going to tell me what to do?

After 4 years of living in the projects, we were told there would be inspections to move residents out into brand new condos so the projects could be torn down. That's how bad it was. When the letter came with the date for our apartment to be inspected, I cleaned every nook and cranny, windows and all. I had never prayed so hard to God. I prayed for him to move us out of that project, and He did. Finally, we got the news that we were selected to move into the new condos on the other side of town, and finally, things were looking up.

Chapter Three

Surviving to Thriving

While things were looking up on the outside, inside, I was still a wreck while going to church. Finally, after 3-4 years of fighting and seemingly doing no good because it kept coming back, I gave in to the voices in my head. I began to wonder what it would be like to be with a woman and party all the time. It became so intense I couldn't fight it anymore. People in the church were making innuendos, voices speaking to me saying the same thing. Finally, I gave in at age 21. I was now grown and would live life on my own terms. I stayed home on Sundays and watched football.

Sundays became a chill at-home day. Eight years into living a lesbian lifestyle, I was hurt, jobless, and tired of Connecticut, so I up and moved to Florida. 1998 September 7, I rode up in an Amtrak bus to St. Petersburg, Florida, where I would live for the next 18 years. In those years, I made friends, I had more heartbreak and up and downs. Sunday's were still my hang-out days. It was a blistering ninety-plus degree outside, and my friends and I had gone to the famous hotel/club in the city. One Sunday was different than all the others. As my friends and I arrived at the club entrance, an outside courtyard with a pool, tiki bar, D.J booth, and food stand, out of nowhere came a woman who said "Hi" in a very soft voice. "She said can I talk to you for just a moment? It won't take long". "I just want to tell you about Jesus." In my mind, I'm like, I need to get rid of this lady real fast, so I turned to her and said, "LADY, I CAN TELL YOU SOMETHING ABOUT JESUS," hoping it would scare her off. Well, it didn't. She stood there and said, "I just want you to know that Jesus loves you."

Then the woman was gone just as quick as she had appeared. I got my party on like nothing had even happened. Looking back in retrospect, I believe she was an angel sent by God. I liked going to this club to party on Sundays because they always had celebrity entertainers, so I continued to go. One Sunday my friends had other plans, so I went alone. When I arrived, I sat on a bench. As I sat there, a boy with a leather skirt, leather boots up to his knees, chains hanging around his torso from his shoulders to his waist walked past me. I saw a flash of HELL, and I said, "God if I am supposed to be doing what you've called me to do, why am I out here"? I got up and left. A few days later, as I was asleep in my dark bedroom with blackout drapes, because I liked sleeping in pitch blackness, so much so I couldn't even see my hand in front of my face, God himself came to the window of my bedroom as I slept. I felt a rumbling and tried to get up from the bed, but I couldn't. I was pinned. The voice of God said to me, "GET BACK IN CHURCH. GET BACK IN CHURCH."

It was that deep thunderous voice of God like in the movie The Ten Commandments when God is talking to Moses. I was so scared once I could get up, I ran straight to the bathroom and turned on the light switch. The bulb was 100 watts (catch that in the spirit). I stood there with my heart pumping so hard as if I had run a marathon. I stood there looking at the window as if God was going to say something else. He said nothing more, so I caught my breath, my heart rate went back to normal, and as I went back to bed, I said, "yes, Lord." I slept like a baby. It was the most peaceful sleep I had.

A couple of Sundays went by, and it was Monday morning, and my coworkers said to me, "Stace, what are you doing this Sunday?" I said, "nothing, probably watching football." She said, "you wanna go to during lunch? She herself was living a lesbian lifestyle. It wasn't as if I didn't know; spirits know each other. After a few months, I had this conversation with God, "Lord, if I'm going to get back in church, I'm not going to be Baptist because they are allowed to live any kind of way." I'm not going to be Church of God in Christ because they have a lot of homosexuals, and it seems to be ok. I'm not going to be non-denominational because they don't know what they want to be. So, it's going to be the 4th Sunday. My co-works says to me, "this Sunday, I'm not going to my church. I'm going to Ms. Pearl's church. Do you still want to go?" I said, "yes." So we went. It's the fall of 2005.

We arrive and walk into the vestibule. It's a large church, so I was looking for the pictures of the forefathers of the house, but there weren't any. Then, suddenly, I felt a cool breeze blow by me. I was like, whew, I never felt that before in any church I had ever attended. Finally, the door I was standing in front of opened, and I saw no usher, but I began to walk through the door and to the right and came to an open pew. I look down the aisle, and I see the usher at the bottom of the ramp with a huge smile on her face that I will never forget. The lead singer was singing her heart out, and the keyboardist was rocking the keys.

I placed my purse on the pew. I thought to myself, this is a church, how I remembered it when I was young. They were jammin' for Jesus! So, I began attending the jammin' for Jesus church (not the church's actual name) for the next few months, and on January 1, 2006, I joined on a Sunday New Year's Day morning. I was taken to the fellowship hall, where I met with Minister over the New Members Department. He asked if I was saved, I said no. He walked me through the sinners' prayer, and I began a journey with Jesus. I attended every other Sunday that I had off from work and weeknights. It was a whole new beginning in life for me. I attended the new members class and graduated with a certificate. I was asked if I wanted to be baptized, I was scared to life, but I did it anyway. When I came up out of the water, it was as if a ton of bricks was lifted up off of me. I felt refreshed.

In my new refreshing life, doors began to open for me, and I joined the Housekeeping and Caregiving ministries. I was promoted on my job to a supervisor and started bible college. I completed the first and the second year. Learning about my walk with Jesus was so refreshing. I was learning things I had never heard before from the Bible. My mind was being transformed little by little. Here is when I finally verbalized the trauma of being raped and molested as a child and not wanting to ever have a relationship with a man. I became curious about being with a woman. I started living a lesbian lifestyle when I left the church at 21. If I was going to go to hell, I would have fun and not go from the church pew was my thinking in 1990.

I was taken through the process of calling out the names of those who had sexually abused me and forgiving them, and being delivered from the trauma and pain of it all.

Many deliverance services took place, and I would find myself getting up off the floor after having hands laid on me by my pastor and being free from bondages that helped me captive. The foundation of Jesus was being laid out under my feet like concrete for a sidewalk. God's word is a lamp unto my feet..., Psalm 119:105 KJV.

My hunger for God increased as I read His word and talked with Him in prayer. One Sunday morning, I walked into Sunday School, and the Minister was ready to begin class. He opened up in prayer and began to teach. As he was teaching, he gave an example of how God had brought conviction to his heart when he would pray for the club to be shut down across from his employment. He said he had to change his prayer. He said, "It went from Lord shut down the club across the street to Lord save souls in that club and then shut it down." I was in shock.

It was the same club I was sitting in every Sunday evening. I sat in complete amazement how God took a man I never knew, had him praying for my soul salvation, and then brought me (the manifestation of his prayer). He never witnessed to me. We had never even met before. It was a totally divine appointment. I had only been going there about three to six months when he shared his story of God convicting his heart. It took me until Wednesday night Bible study before I could actually tell him that I was the one he had been praying for in that club. I was the very soul he had asked God to save. I was the manifestation of his prayers.

Chapter Four

Seeing God

It's April 2009, and Spring is in effect in Florida as SUMMER is in most places. I'm coming down 9th street, where there is a brand new crosswalk I was unaware of, and it has people in it crossing the street. The truck in front of me comes to a complete stop, and I have to think fast because I didn't know why he stopped. I see the back of his truck as I'm slamming on my brakes. I say I can't hit him in the back it will be my fault, so I slide to the left to slow the car down to keep from hitting this truck in the back as the driver is looking at me from his rearview mirror, wanting me to hit him in the rear. As I slide to the left, a car is pulling up next to me to come to a stop as well. Our cars make contact, and instantly I hear the Lord say, "THE NEXT ONE IS GOING

TO BE WORST." There were only minor scratches on her car and mine as well.

God can not lie, on June 21, 2009, Sunday, I attended the first Father's Day event, and it was grandeur! At the conclusion, I was on my way home on the highway doing the speed limit of 65, and all of a sudden, I was being T-boned by another automobile. I look over, and things feel like moving in slow motion. To my right, I see the car's grill that is hitting me smile like the face of the devil. I SCREAMED JEEESSSUUUS! My hands are frozen on the steering wheel, and the HANDS OF GOD came from the sky and into my car and began to steer the wheel until it reached my hands and kept turning the wheel.

I was doing a 360 in the middle of the highway, I saw traffic coming at me, and I

SCREAMED JEEESSSUUUS AGAIN, and my car came to a complete stop. Instantly the Holy Ghost said to me, "do not panic, your car is still running, and your radio is still on, back up."

Without hesitation or even looking back, I backed the car ultimately onto the shoulder of the highway and turned the ignition off. I looked over to the left, and I saw the car that hit me trickle down the highway, but there was another car following it. I sat there, and it felt like an eternity. I saw my church family drive by me doing 65 miles an hour, leaving the same event. My Bible was in the front passenger seat, and it didn't move one bit, but my phone was thrown somewhere, and I couldn't find it. I sat there and fell into a trance. I looked over to my right, outside of my car door. I saw JESUS standing there! All I can do is look. I can't speak or move. Then I hear a screaming voice, "are you ok? Are you ok" "I saw the whole thing happen," the guy swirled to keep from hitting me, and he hit you' said the young man? He had his cell phone in his hand, calling the police. I said, "can I use your phone, please?" He handed it to me, and I called the only number I had memorized in this cell phone age. I called my spiritual sister, my angel on earth, from my new birth in Christ. She parked in front of me on the highway shoulder when she arrived. She jumped out and swiftly walked over to the passenger side of my car, and all I heard was I NEED HELP!!! The ambulance arrived and asked me if I was ok. I said yes. He said we need to take you to the hospital. They loaded me in the ambulance, and off to the hospital we went. Once I was done with x-rays, my Spiritual Mom was there with my spiritual sister, a licensed nurse. I felt no pain. I suffered no injury. The Protection of God's hands saved my life.

God had also prepared transportation for me, being as though my car was totaled. Every time I would drive to the church, I would see this car sitting there and wonder whose car it was, not knowing it would be soon mine. Someone had donated it to the church. Some of you may know that following Christ will cost you something. I had no idea I would go through such happenings. Nevertheless, I'm Still Standing in Christ!!!

Chapter Five

On Assignment

Soon after having gone through two car accidents and walking away unhurt from both of them, still loving God, I was promoted again on my job. I was promoted to management and worked at the local children's hospital. Still working in the caregiving ministry, I was assigned to look after one of our newest member's daughter, who was two years old at the time and in need of a heart transplant. The Pastor prayed and prophesied that she would get a new heart and be running around with the other children again.

The testing and being placed on a donor's list were two months. Unfortunately, a little baby boy had passed away, and his parents had the tough decision to donate his organs. His heart went for testing, and it was a match. The surgery was performed, the heart was not rejected, and accurate to the prophecy, the little girl is now running and playing with the other children after 2 years of doctor appointments and follow-up testing. As of right now, she is 8 years old and going strong. I nicked named her **MIRACLE!** She is truly a **MIRACLE!!!!**

ASSIGNMENT #2

After completing assignment one, I was transferred to Naples, Florida, a two-and-a-half-hour drive south of St. Petersburg. I was given my new work location, the North Campus of Naples Community Hospital. The Lord spoke to me and told me where I should live, and He said, "Ft. Myers". So, I ventured out to start looking after being in Naples for a month, and everywhere I looked was Million dollar homes or places that said I make too much money, so the Lord reminded me that He said I was to live in Ft. Myers. So, I was wasting my time looking elsewhere. So, I drove over to Ft. Myers the following weekend. It's a 45-minute drive, and I said, God, I'm getting off the first exit that says Ft. Myers. It was exit 136, so I came to a couple of nice apartment complexes, and I stopped in one and asked if they had availability and the required documentation I would need.

So, after completing the necessary papers and Paying deposits and a month's rent, I move in a week later. It's now a month, and I'm getting used to the 45-minute drive to and from work and loving having every weekend off. Some weekends I would drive the 2 hours to St. Petersburg for church, and some weekends I would just say home and get in the FACE of God at home. This one particular Saturday, I was basking in the GLORY, and the Lord said: "Go to the hospital and pray for Ms. Johnson." I said, "ok." I get there down, and Ms. Johnson is one of my staff admitted as a patient. So, I walk in and talk with Ms. Johnson, and I pray for her and head back to Ft. Myers. It pays to obey God.

The next day being Sunday, I received a call from my boss saying beginning tomorrow (Monday), I would no longer report to the north campus hospital, but I would report to the downtown hospital. They had hired a new manager from the hospital, and he couldn't stay at that location, so they had switched the two of us.

So, Monday morning, I reported to the downtown location and began another new chapter. I am given the second shift from 3pm-12:30am. I have another new boss to get to know and an Assistant Director to get to know. Upon my arrival, the Assistant Direct was on vacation. He and I shared an office, so just imagine going on vacation and coming back to your office with a new person sharing your space. What an experience it was. A week goes by, and I get a call from the supervisor who worked with me at the north campus hospital, and she says, "Stacey, Ms. Johnson said thank you for praying for her. She is out of the hospital and doing well"! I said, "Praise God"!! God is good!

The assist became my thorn in the flesh, The Director has become very aggressive, and I'm like Lord, what is going on. I get a call into my director's office, and he says, "have a seat" I sit, and he begins to tell me about his being forced to retire. He's 65. The Bible says A man's gift maketh room for him and bringeth him before great men. Proverbs 18:16 King James Version. As I soon realize that this will be a golden opportunity to plant seeds, I sit and listen very attentively to what's being said and what the Holy Ghost will have to say through me to him. After letting me know of his being forced out, he also let me know his replacement was coming soon. The Holy Ghost had me reassure him that when God closes a door, He will open a window, and He also led me to tell him about the saving grace of Jesus Christ. He looked me square in the eyes and said, "I'll have you know I grew up a Baptist Boy" I smiled real hard at him and said, "then you know God will never leave you nor forsake you." He said, "yeah, I know, but I'm still scared. I have a terrible gambling habit, and I have no money. I may have also scheduled for surgery, and my insurance will run out". Then he remembered the company was giving him his vacation time plus sick time before his insurance ran out. I prayed for him and his wellbeing as he sat in his office, and it was time to get back to work and get my staff upon their scheduled areas of work for the night. He said, "Thank you!" Inside, I was thanking God for the opportunity.

The seed was planted, and I left it up to God to increase. As our director's time came to depart and have his surgery, we wished him well. A week later, he was back at the hospital as a patient, and during my rounds, I would visit him. Upon the very first visit, I walked into his room to find him reading his Bible. We talked about his procedure, how things were going with him, and how his hope in the Lord grew. After his surgery, he would be praying or reading his word during my rounds on his floor at the hospital. Soon after, he was discharged, my assignment was completed, and I moved on.

Conclusion

By the grace of God and through deliverance ministry, God healed me from unforgiveness, offense, and past hurts. As long as you live, there will be painful situations that arise and some seemingly out of nowhere that will bring you to a choice of I trust God and live or stay here in pain and anguish and slowly die. It's your God-given choice, and He will not override your decisions. He's a gentleman. He waits to be invited into your heart, life, and whatever situation you may be going through, even at this present time. It's up to you to invite Him in.

He did it and is doing it for me. That's why I love Him so. He can do it for you as well. Just in case you may have missed the moral of the journey: No matter what has happened to you in life, no matter where God found you in life, God can mend the broken pieces of your life and make a beautiful masterpiece. Once you receive Christ as your personal Lord and Savior, you become a new creature in Christ Jesus, old things are passed away and behold, all things become new. This makes you an instant candidate for all the promises of God and to be used as a free agent of God.

I write this book in the hope of helping others journey through pain that life may have brought your way. Do know that in Christ, there is healing and deliverance from every form of pain. There is hope, help, and healing for those who've suffered or are currently suffering in silence. Reach out to God, and He will direct your path. You, too, can go from surviving to thriving in Jesus. Welcome to the army of God, forward march, soldier!

Closing Remarks

As for my mother lived the last eighteen years of her life saved and served in ministry at her home church. Once she did so, there was no need to bring up the past, so Mom died never knowing the things that happened to me, but can I tell you that God is so gracious He gave me a spiritual Mom who I can share all of the sexual abuse, mental anguish, arrested development with. She prays with me and for me. She is my Ma, Apostle Rosemary Haynes of House of Prayer in Stratford, CT. I am grateful for the village it's taken to get me where I am today, and the best is yet to come.

Contacts

For all your bulk purchases, comments, questions, or book signing events, please email me at:

staceyt113@yahoo.co.uk

or your can visit my Social Media page at:

Facebook @ stacey.tur